Gardens

Growing a
Garden

by Mari Schuh

Consulting Editor: Gail Saunders-Smith, PhD

Consultant: Sarah Pounders
Education Specialist, National Gardening Association

CAPSTONE PRESS
a capstone imprint

Pebble Books are published by Capstone Press,
151 Good Counsel Drive, P.O. Box 669, Mankato, Minnesota 56002.
www.capstonepress.com

Copyright © 2010 by Capstone Press, a Capstone imprint.
All rights reserved. No part of this publication may be reproduced in whole or in
part, or stored in a retrieval system, or transmitted in any form or by any means,
electronic, mechanical, photocopying, recording, or otherwise, without
written permission of the publisher. For information regarding permission, write
to Capstone Press, 151 Good Counsel Drive, P.O. Box 669, Dept. R, Mankato,
Minnesota 56002.

Printed in the United States of America in North Mankato, Minnesota
092009
005618CGS10

Books published by Capstone Press are manufactured with paper
containing at least 10 percent post-consumer waste.

Library of Congress Cataloging-in-Publication Data
Schuh, Mari C., 1975–
    Growing a garden / by Mari Schuh.
    p. cm. — (Pebble books. Gardens)
    Summary: "Simple text and photographs present an overview of growing
a garden" — Provided by publisher.
    Includes bibliographical references and index.
    ISBN 978-1-4296-3984-2 (library binding)
    ISBN 978-1-4296-4842-4 (paperback)
    1. Gardening — Juvenile literature. I. Title. II. Series: Pebble (Mankato, Minn.).
Gardens.
SB457.S377 2010
635 — dc22   2009025593

Note to Parents and Teachers

The Gardens set supports national science standards related to life science.
This book describes and illustrates growing a garden. The images support
early readers in understanding the text. The repetition of words and
phrases helps early readers learn new words. This book also introduces
early readers to subject-specific vocabulary words, which are defined
in the Glossary section. Early readers may need assistance to read some
words and to use the Table of Contents, Glossary, Read More, Internet
Sites, and Index sections of the book.

The author dedicates this book to her good friend and expert organic
gardener, Chris De Santis of Somers, Wisconsin.

Table of Contents

Getting Started

It's spring
and the soil is warm.
Let's find a sunny spot
to start the garden.

Preparing and Planting

Loosen the soil with a hoe. Loose soil holds more water for your plants.

Add nutrients to the soil
with compost.
Nutrients help plants grow.

Even out the soil
with a rake.

Seed packets say
how and where
to plant your seeds.
Plant vegetable seeds
in rows.

Watering and Weeding

When the soil feels dry,

it's time to water the garden.

Water in early morning.

Then more water

soaks into the soil.

Gently pull weeds
and their roots
out of the ground.
Weed the garden
every week.

Picking Time

Gather your vegetables
and fruits from the garden.
Pick them when
they are ripe.

Next Year

Clean up your garden before winter. In spring, it's time to plant again.

Glossary

compost — a mixture of rotted leaves, vegetables, and manure that is added to soil to make it richer

hoe — a gardening tool with a long handle and a thin blade

nutrient — something needed by plants to stay strong and healthy

ripe — ready to be picked or eaten

root — the part of a plant that grows underground

weed — an unwanted plant; weeds block the sunlight and use water and nutrients needed by garden plants.

Read More

Morris, Ting, and Neil Morris. *Growing Things*. Sticky Fingers. Mankato, Minn.: Sea-to-Sea, 2007.

Schuh, Mari C. *Tools for the Garden*. Gardens. Mankato, Minn.: Capstone Press, 2010.

Whitehouse, Patricia. *Plant and Prune*. Tool Kit. Vero Beach, Fla.: Rourke, 2007.

Internet Sites

FactHound offers a safe, fun way to find Internet sites related to this book. All of the sites on FactHound have been researched by our staff.

Here's all you do:

Visit *www.facthound.com*

FactHound will fetch the best sites for you!

Index

Word Count: 127
Grade: 1
Early-Intervention Level: 13

Credits
Jenny Marks, editor; Heidi Thompson, designer; Marcie Spence, media
researcher; Eric Manske, production specialist; Sarah Schuette, photo stylist;
Marcy Morin, photo scheduler

Photo Credits
All photos by Capstone Studio/Karon Dubke